photo by taylor dennis photography

YOU ARE MY SUN.
MY MOON.
AND ALL OF MY STARS.

BRIGGSY

www.michaelbriggs.com.au

THE TEAM

EDITOR & CO-FOUNDER
Tara Baker

CREATIVE DIRECTOR & CO-FOUNDER
Arlia Hassell

CONTRIBUTING PHOTOGRAPHERS
Madeline Kate, Talitha Crawford Photography, Eager Hearts Photography, Coral Dove Photography, Tahnee Jade Photography, Robyn Nicole Film and Photo, Georgia Wiggs Photography, Stories By Bianca, Ridhwaan Moolla, Emily Howlett Photography, Kamra Fuller Photography, Cloud Catcher Studio

FRONT COVER IMAGE
Tahnee Jade Photography
www.tahneejadephotography.com

BACK COVER IMAGE
Ridhwaan Moolla
www.ridhwaanmoolla.com

EDITORIAL CONTRIBUTIONS
Caroline & Nergis, Shannon Stent, Kitty Kulman, Kate Faoro

SUBMISSIONS
www.dancingwithher.com/submityourstory

ADVERTISING & WHOLESALE ENQUIRIES
partnerships@dancingwithher.com

DANCING WITH HER
P.O. Box 609
Coolangatta, QLD, 4225
Australia

JOIN OUR COMMUNITY
www.dancingwithher.com

facebook.com/dancingwithher
instagram.com/dancingwithher
pinterest.com/dancingwithher

Dancing With Her acknowledges the Australian Aboriginal and Torres Strait Islander peoples of this nation. We acknowledge the people of the Bundjalung Nation whose Land on which our company is located and where we primarily conduct our business. We pay our respects to Ancestors and Elders, past, present and emerging. Dancing With Her is committed to honouring Australian Aboriginal and Torres Strait Islander peoples unique cultural and spiritual relationships to the land, waters and seas and their rich contribution to society.

AMELIA & KATE

Millawa, Australia

12

PETRA & SHARI

Byron Bay, Australia

22

NICOLETTE & SAMANTHA

New York, United States of America

32

EMMA & NICOLE

Drysdale, Australia

46

ERICA & LEAH

St Kilda, Australia

60

JAMIE & MADELEINE

Kaukapakapa, New Zealand

68

JESSICA & SARAH

Carlsruhe, Australia

84

CLEO & LIV

Kirra, Australia

98

Emily Howlett

P H O T O G R A P H Y

fun . natural . relaxed

www.howlettphotographyweddings.com

emilyhowlettphotography@live.com.au

HELLO

Welcome to Volume Five

As we write this, sitting together side by side, we can't help but have thoughts consumed by what today's date means. Today is the 50th anniversary of the Stonewall riots. We have taken a moment to remember those, particularly the gender diverse women of color, who took those first steps in fighting for a more inclusive and accepting future and we are so grateful that they did. Without those fearless warriors, it is hard to imagine just where the world would be right now.

We also want to congratulate Taiwan, the very first country across Asia to have marriage equality made legal. We have so much hope that this will be a catalyst for change across Asia, a change we know so many of our readers are waiting for.

Inside this issue of our magazine, you're going to find some of the most incredible love stories that have crossed our inbox. Our cover lovers, Amelia and Ellie share their wedding dress dramas and last minute decision to switch up the outfits. Caroline and Nergis share their curiosity around culture and their pride in being an Islamic and Catholic, inter-racial couple.

We were intrigued by Nicolette and Samantha's almost Game of Thrones inspired New York wedding, in a castle[!], and fell head over heels for Jessica and Sarah, two lovers who met like a lot of our readers do - on a dancefloor after midnight.

We hope you love this volume and turn every page up until the very last page with a heart full of joy.

Thank you, as always, for your support in helping us bring Dancing With Her to life. We pinch ourselves every day wondering how we got so lucky to have built a strong and connected community of LGBTQ+ lovers around us.

Love,
Arlia & Tara

Want to get your favourite people together, celebrate your engagement and do a spot of wedding planning? If you're in Brisbane [or willing to travel - it will be worth the trip!] A Darling Affair is set to be the modern wedding fair of the year! With a handpicked selection of the very best wedding pros that Byron Bay to the Sunshine Coast have to offer, it's creative, fun and best for couples who think outside the box. We'll see you there!

Here are all the details:
Sunday 27th October 11-3pm
The Warehouse Brisbane
@adarlingaffair

www.adarlingaffair.com

Harper Cosmetics was born following a long time love affair with quality makeup containing high pigments and a range of color options.

Whether you're doing your own wedding day makeup, or you're looking for a new everyday eyeshadow palette, these palettes are really creamy on the eye and don't stain the skin. They've become an everyday staple for us!

Also, their lipsticks- they will stay on all day and they're not drying at all. Their mid-tone nudes are our favorites, Chubby and Nirvana for everyday and Womanizer or Bora Bora when we're feeling fun!

www.harpercosmetics.com.au

For the last decade, Vale Jewelry has established itself as the go-to brand for both modern and alternative couples looking for bespoke engagement rings and wedding bands.

Vale Jewelry use recycled 14K and 18K gold and responsibly-mined diamonds and gems, with the belief of creating beautiful pieces through sustainable sourcing and ethical practices - something that is so, so important to us.

Each piece is handcrafted and really afforable, some simple rings come in under $500. And, the best part- they ship across the globe.

www.shopvale.com

We are huge fans of natural alternatives and Rohr Remedies tick all the boxes with their Australian bush medicine meets dermatological science approach.

You won't find any nasties inside these products, and everything is palm oil and cruelty-free. The collection of plants used in the products is also environmentally sustainable and the team at Rohr Remedies work with local Indigenous land owners to create every single product in their range.

We no longer leave the house with the Gumbi Gumbi lip balm- a new favorite!

www.rohrremedy.com

Looking for the perfect gift for your wedding party VIP's? Maybe these Maison de Sabré clutches, that'll be both handy on the wedding day and then can be used for forever, are the perfect gift?!

They're sleek and stylish, crafted from quality bovine leather and a matching removable cardholder which comes in handy. Also, each one is individually pressed and personalized with a momogram of your choice- we'd suggest adding initals for a really personal touch.

We're also giving away a personalized phone case and clutch worth $228.

www.maisondesabre.com
www.dancingwithher.com/win

The Lesser Bear is a socially conscious company that uses natural and foraged dye materials to create beautiful ribbons and textiles, while simultaneously doing its part to engage through acts of kindness and generosity.

Kate, the Designer, and maker behind The Lesser Bear creates silk ribbons, handspun twines, table linens and other details for weddings. All textiles are dyed by Kate, in her studio, using flowers and plants. Lesser Bear products are made with care and creativity to will help you create your dream wedding and celebrate your love- totally unique to your love tale.

www.thelesserbear.com

AMELIA & ELLIE

PHOTOGRAPHY BY MADELINE KATE

www.madelinekate.com.au

MILLAWA, AUSTRALIA

On a family trip to the US, Amelia and Ellie decided to venture off to New York for some time together. Amelia had taken a ring over to America intending to propose, however, after a dinner date she turned around to find Ellie down on one knee. It was completely unexpected but pure. The very next day Amelia proposed back with the ring she had also been carrying around.

For the first six months of wedding planning, Amelia, who is generally the organized planner of the couple, was strong spirited. She believed in herself to plan every detail. Multiple meltdowns ensued and they both decided that hiring a wedding planner would be best. It turns out that hiring a planner would come to be the best decision they made.

From day one, a wedding that was natural and relaxed was paramount. While they had dreamt of a rustic style wedding, the dream was solidified from the moment they first saw Brown Brothers. The barn and the ceremony venue brought to life everything the couple had visualized.

With a wedding planner in place, Amelia and Ellie decided on minimal DIY projects. They opted for downloadable templates for all of their stationery and Ellie, who is a trained carpenter, constructed the arbor that they would be married under and each of the wooden blocks that would scatter across the tables and display menus.

Each bride-to-be wanted to wear a dress. Amelia's experience was right out of your favorite rom-com. She attended a sample sale, and it was intense. There was yelling, dress stealing and at one point Amelia was close to tears. She left with a dress, but a few months down the track admitted to herself that it wasn't the one.

The second dress was purchased from a showroom, with her maid-of-honor, godmother and champagne. It was the experience that she'd dreamt about.

Ellie initially wanted to wear a dress and brought one for herself. But, as someone who rarely wears dresses, she decided just days before the wedding that she would be more comfortable in a shirt and pants.

When finding wedding vendors, Amelia and Ellie wanted the day to run smoothly so chose to ask each vendor for their recommendation. It meant that the day was brought to life by vendors who really enjoyed working together. Additional to this, they spent time going over each vendors social media accounts, making sure that their values aligned with theirs.

When the wedding day came around, it was a mixture of chaos, calm, nerves and overwhelming excitement. Spending the night before apart, the anticipation of the first look made light by the support of their bridesmaid's and bridesmen.

The moment they first saw each other, the build-up of nerves turned into pure excitement and that flowed through the ceremony and on to the reception where, alongside their favorite people, the couple laughed, cried, drank and danced all night.

For the newlyweds, one of their favorite moments was at the reception where they took a moment to step back and take it all in; appreciating the fact that everyone they loved was in one room. The wedding day flew by, one surreal blur, and Amelia and Ellie are thankful that they have that memory to always reflect on.

Cake Miss Ladybird Cakes | **Catering** Brown Brothers Winery | **Celebrant** Wendy Does Weddings | **Ceremony Venue & Reception Venue** Brown Brothers | **Cinematographer** Anchored Cinema | **Desserts** Cupcake Central | **Engagement Rings** The Wooden Circle | **Entertainment** DJ BEX Cavanagh **Event Planner & Stylist** Aster & Rose | **Florist** Poppy's Getting Married | **Gown Designer** Grace Loves Lace | **Makeup** Tahlia Tropeano- Makeup Artistry & Lashes | **Order of Events** Sign Heaven & Fifth Paper Co. | **Desserts** Cupcake Central | **Photographer** Madeline Kate Photography | **Place Cards, Menus, Table Numbers, Seating Chart & Welcome Sign** Hope Street Creative | **Stationery** Paradise Invitations | **Wedding Favors** Brown Brothers Prosecco Jam | **Wedding Rings** Michael Hill

THE FIRST LOOK
Words by Shelby Kate

I still remember the first time that I saw her.

It was just after midnight. Usually, I would be the type that told you that nothing, and I mean nothing, good ever comes after midnight, but this night was different.

She was wearing a pair of black jeans, dirty Converse sneakers and a tee that said 'queer' in rainbow letters. She had gold glitter under her eyes and her long blonde hair pulled back in a high pony. She was moving her body in rhythm to the music with confidence. Quite literally dancing like no one was watching.

I felt intimidated but intrigued. She was beautiful and I needed to know more.

Heart racing, palms sweating, I reached for my beer bottle, grabbed my two friends and head straight out the door. I needed a minute to collect my thoughts. With liquid courage on board, I asked my friends if they'd also seen the beautiful women on the dancefloor? No, they reponded, apparently it was just me.

After a little convincing, and a reminder that I had nothing to lose, I was pushed back into the bar and told to make a move.

It's been a whirlwind since then. We danced and kissed that night. We parted ways after exchanging numbers and a long embrace. She met my family a few weeks later, we adopted a puppy, Oscar, and moved in together right after that. And now, we are married.

I thought there wasn't a moment that would ever feel similar to what I felt that first time I saw her. That was until our wedding day.

Having a first look seemed non-traditional, but growing in popularity. We had seen incredible emotional images across social media of two lovers seeing each other for the very first time on their wedding day and we decided that it was something that we wanted to have captured too.

It's one thing to feel the emotion, but another to have the moment captured in a way that freezes time.

We both felt shy about being the center of attention at the ceremony and felt that having a private moment together just before was perfect.

The anticipation was immense. There is no real way to explain the feeling unless you've experienced it. It is a wild concoction of nerves and excitement, pure joy and surrealness.

Brought together blindfolded by our photographer, we were placed back to back and locked our hands together. It was a sudden wave of calm. She was there and we were together. She whispered to me; 'are you ready sweetheart?'

Palms sweaty, heart racing, just like that first time we saw each other, I replied; 'I love you.'

On our photographer's cue, we each turned.

It was the first time in my life that I felt completely speechless. I felt tears well up almost immediately as I covered my mouth with both hands. She looked incredible. I had no words.

I felt pure elation. Just as I had stumbled to find a 'yes' between tears when she had asked me to be her wife nearly two years ago, I stumbled to find the words to tell her just how beautiful she was.

I don't remember what I said. The photographs tell me that not a whole lot of words probably did come out, rather a whole lot of tears and a smile bigger than a kid who has just got off their favorite ride at the fair. I look happy, thrilled in fact, that the women standing right in front of me is set to be my wife in a matter of minutes.

Having that moment captured is something we will both forever cherish. It was intimate and raw. We were both unaware of our photographer snapping away, completely wrapped up in one another and what we were about to embark on together. They are photographs that mean the world to us and tell the story of two lovers who hadn't seen each other since breakfast on one of the most important days of their lives. Two women who are choosing to commit to a marriage together, starting a new chapter of their lives intertwined.

PETRA & SHARI

PHOTOGRAPHY BY TALITHA CRAWFORD PHOTOGRAPHY
www.talithacrawfordphotography.com

BYRON BAY, AUSTRALIA

welcome
TO THE
WEDDING OF
petra & shari

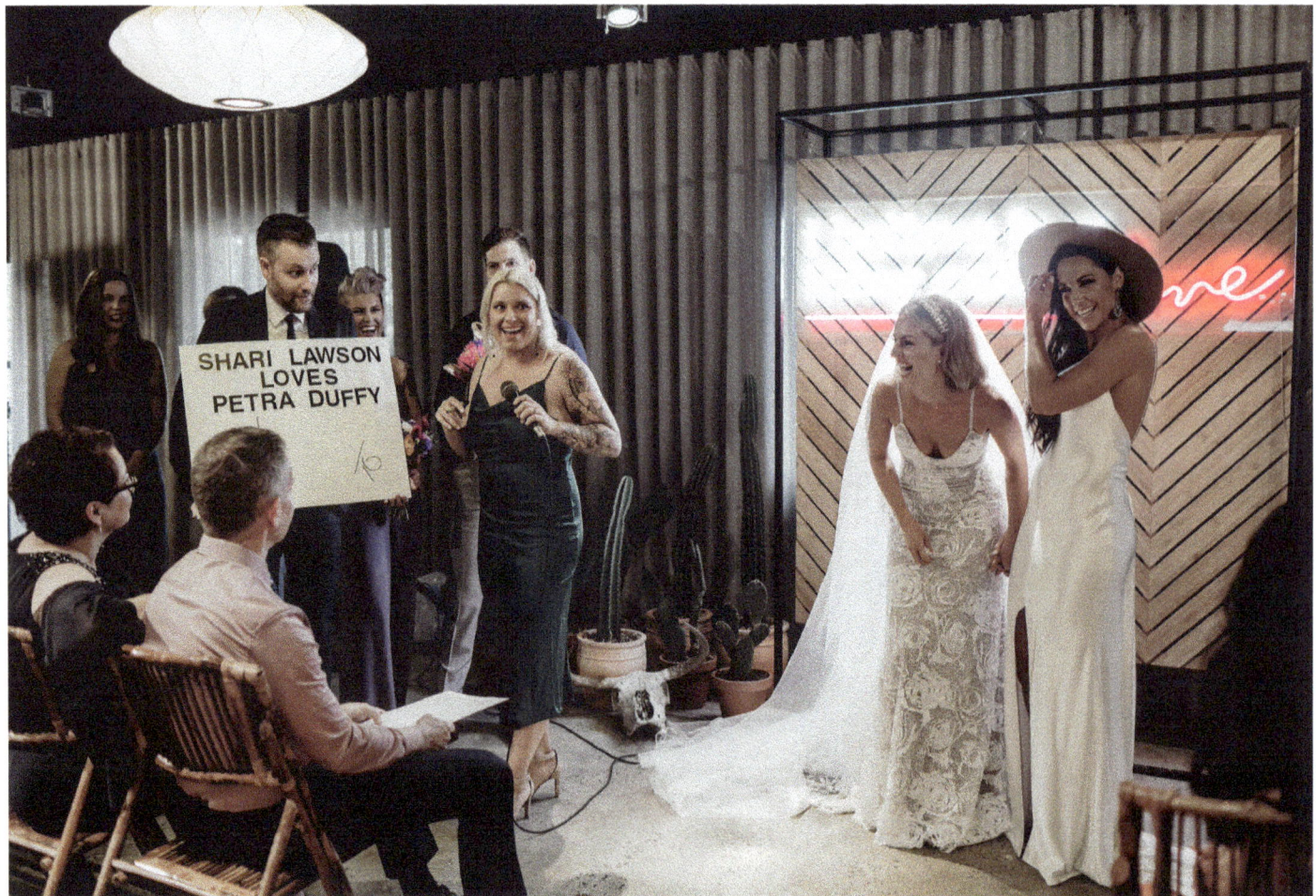

SHARI LAWSON
LOVES
PETRA DUFFY

Petra and Shari are two adventurous souls that first met on at a Brisbane nightclub. Sparks did not fly initially, in fact, it would take a few years for timing to be right and butterflies to suddenly develop. When they did, it wasn't long before they could not get enough of one another.

A rather long engagement of nearly two and a half years was always on the cards. It completely eliminated any wedding stress leaving plenty of time to finesse details and secure all of their preferred vendors.

As a couple who love nothing more than exploring the world and immersing themselves in new cultures, a destination wedding vibe was essential. Byron Bay had always been on the radar because of its laid back vibe and stunning scenery- it was the perfect destination close to home.

For Shari, who had dreamt of her wedding dress moment her entire life, it was hard to decide on just one dress for the wedding day. Petra had initially planned on wearing a two-piece, until she totally surprised herself falling for the first gown she tried on. It was the hat that took a little longer to get perfect. After pestering Shari for months on end over finding a hat, dedicating more than one hundred hours scrolling the internet for 'the one' and purchasing four different variations, Petra finally settled on the two that would bring the entire outfit to life.

Focusing on vibrant colors and inspired by Aztec vibes, Petra and Shari's wedding came together with the help of family and friends. Cacti were collected in the weeks leading up to the day; Petra's Mum helped hand make over thirty cushions in an Aztec inspired material that Petra knew was perfect and Shari's Mum and Step Dad drove a rental truck around town picking up random bits and pieces and hired styling.

One friend designed a canvas that was used as a guest book and others put together grazing platters for guests. Even the bouquets were DIY.

The day before the wedding was the only time that the pair had any wedding nerves. A forecast of thunderstorms, and two brides who wanted an outdoor reception and photos by the ocean, was the receipe for pre-wedding breakdown, overcome with emotions.

In a massive seven bedroom beach house, the wedding morning vibe was electric. With 25+ people getting ready together and starting to celebrate what was to come, the nerves around any bad weather parted.

On the day, it rained, a lot. A quick-thinking celebrant moved the arbor, lights, chairs and cacti indoors at the last minute.

With a now indoor ceremony, the vibe quickly turned to one that resembled kids at school who misbehave and become loud and cheeky when lunch is canceled due to weather. It was intimate, moody and a whole heap of fun.

The ceremony was also interactive. A friend turning her speech into a game show about the brides' love story- only she got a few details completely wrong which made it hilarious for both the lovers and their guests.

It couldn't have been more perfect if they had planned it.

And, after some very long and detailed vows that spoke to committing to one another for the rest of their lives, Petra and Shari's celebrant said those few words to make it official; "I now pronounce you mother f@#cking married!"

Bridal Boutique Sphere Collective | **Catering** Culinary Catering | **Celebrant** Paul Voge | **Cinematographer** Rabbit and the Bear | **Crown** Crystal Eclipse Crowns | **Entertainment** DJ Bure Goodwin, Kyle Bryant | **Florist** Persephone Rebel Handmaiden | **Food Cart** Head Over Wheels | **Furniture Hire** The Wedding Shed | **Gelato** Wheel and Spoon | **Gown** Grace Loves Lace, Chosen by One Day Bridal | **H&MU** Jazba Boutique, Miranda Emblem | **Hat** Lack of Color | **Neon** Neon Republic | **Photographer** Talitha Crawford Photography | **Rings** DM Jeweler | **Veil** Grace Loves Lace | **Venue** Secret Garden Byron Bay

LOVE YOUR WEDDING PHOTOGRAPHY
Memories to reflect back on for a lifetime

Wedding photography; aside from the marriage and memories is the one part of your wedding day that will last longer than the dreaded hangover and something that you'll be investing a fair chunk of your wedding day budget into. And, when you open the gallery of photographs eight or so weeks after you've said your commitments and partied 'till the early hours of the morning, you are going to want to open up a gallery of incredible images that take you right back to the day, right?

It can all seem overwhelming at first glance. There are quite literally thousands of photographers to choose from, what they offer is ever different and the prices they charge fluctuate too. But, there are a few things that you can do before you decide on locking in a photographer to help make sure that you love your wedding photography.

Before you start looking, ask people you know who have been married not just for recommendations, but what they wished they had known before they got their final gallery back. Hindsight is such a wonderful thing, you might as well use their experience to your advantage.

Then you'll need to figure out what style you most love. Photographers work in a range of styles, it's art after all. You'll want to look not just at the type of photography but also at the way the images are edited. Art is subjective and so, there will be some styles you adore and others that just aren't for you, and that is totally okay. When you're doing this, don't forget that looking at photographers blogs is important, you'll want to see more than just the 'best images' that are used across social media. Check to see how they capture family members, the wedding day details and the love story.

Once you've narrowed down your favorites, and you've determined that they are within your price range and can do dates that you are looking at, lock in a time to jump on video chat or phone call with them. You'll really want to suss out if the photographer/s is 'your people.'

Your photographer is going to be a huge part of your day. They will be third wheeling while you get ready with your loved ones, they'll be spying on your first look and will be holding back the tears as you let release your heart and say your vows. You'll not just want someone that you can trust, but someone that you vibe with too. If you are a loud and confident couple a photographer that is a little shy might not be the right fit, but for a couple that grimaces at the thought of being the center of attention their gentle and calm nature might be perfect.

If you're marrying outside in the middle of the day, you'll want a photographer who is comfortable shooting in the outdoors, and full sun if applicable. If you're having a moody indoor wedding you'll need someone who is comfortable shooting in low light. If a photographer that you're considering has shot at the venue that you're getting married at, it is okay to ask for some examples from the wedding, but use them only to guide your decision making - your wedding is going to be unique to whatever they might have shot before.

Once you've locked someone in and you are getting closer to the big day, your photographer will usually ask you if there are certain photographs that you want, particularly around group shots. This a good chance to let your photographer know who is going to be there, and if there is anything important they need to know; like that parents are separated and you might want family shots from each side of the family taken separately.

On the day, let your photographer guide you; in most cases, they have done this a few more times than you have and they will know what works and what doesn't. Make sure they are aware of the timeline of the day and let them get on with what you've hired them to do- capture your love story.

And, when the day rolls around for you to open that wedding gallery over a wine or tea one evening, enjoy every moment of reliving the experience.

NICOLETTE & SAMANTHA

PHOTOGRAPHY BY EAGER HEARTS PHOTOGRAPHY
www.eagerheartsphotography.com

NEW YORK, UNITED STATES OF AMERICA

They began dating back in college, just a few months before graduation. They were in the same group of friends but were in and out of other relationships throughout most of college. It wasn't until they realized that they had so many things in common, and were actually really attracted to each other that they finally went on a date. Both Nicolette and Samantha knew from that night their lives had changed. It was love at first date.

Over the next four years, they moved in together, went through two master degrees and six jobs, adopted three cats, coped through three deaths and two major family crises, went on half a dozen vacations and watched every episode of Game of Thrones together. Then, after all that, Nicolette and Samantha decided to make official what they had known since that very first date; that they wanted to spend forever together.

It was important that their wedding reflected every aspect of their lives. These lovers love fantasy; magic and mysticism, the Middle Ages, festivals, cosplay and all things Harry Potter. With pride, the couple attend organized events for fantasy lovers and their wedding day needed to be a representation of just how geeky they are. So the theme was set, they would have a Renaissance-themed wedding day.

The Castel Hotel and Spa in Tarrytown, New York was the perfect host venue to bring to life the theme. The castle, Tudor-inspired, had stone walls and tapestries, exposed beams and dark wooden panels. The Great Hall complete with stained-glass windows.

Being a near complete DIY wedding, Nicolette and Samantha quickly learnt exactly why other couples hire wedding planners. Hours were spent hand-writing notes with quill and ink, stamping wax seals, lugging old wooden chairs and candelabras, and shopping about at conventions

and fairs to find the perfect short sword. Every single detail mattered to the brides-to-be.

Despite limitations, Nicolette and Samantha had the opportunity to achieve everything they had dreamt of with a, carefully selected, dream team of wedding vendors.

In planning, the couple allowed the time and didn't overdo it with getting things done on strict timelines. They shared tasks and made every decision together, as a couple. Dress shopping was no exception, they each wanted to look complimentary and in fantasy theme, but also be comfortable in their own style and personality.

Finding the perfect dress was a 'meant to be' moment. Miraculously, Nicolette and Samantha each found their ideal dresses in the very first bridal shop they visited. A genius bridal consultant remembering two gowns, both from different designers, met all of their requirements and happened to have matching buttons down the back.

And, on a crisp December night, right after sunset, Nicolette and Samantha married.

The ceremony was intimate, with just family and friends surrounding the newlyweds, and the reception a banquet fit for queens. They lounged in their thrones like Cate Blanchett in Elizabeth and were introduced to the reception on a balcony as strings played the Game of Thrones theme song.

Their day was exactly how they had dreamt; epic and unforgettable, the best day of their lives.

Bridal Boutique Seng Couture | **Cake** Candice Gressett | **Entertainment** SPN Events, Michelle Mountain, Autumn Ward | **Floral** Tarrytown Floral Design **H&MU** Angela Boswell | **Officiant** A Joyful Ceremony | **Photography** Eager Hearts Photography | **Rentals** Prop Rentals NY, Regal Candelabra | **Rings** Greenwich St. Jewelers | **Venue** Castle Hotel and Spa | **Videography** Dideo Film and Photography

EMILY SCHUTZ PHOTOGRAPHY
ELOPEMENTS • WEDDINGS • INTIMATE PORTRAITS
WWW.EMILYSCHUTZ.COM

THE PRESSURE OF PERFECT

Why there is no such thing as a 'perfect wedding day'

'It's going to be the best day of my life.' 'I've dreamt of this fairytale since I was a child.' 'I want everything to be perfect.'

There is a real pressure of wedding day perfection. Instagram and Pinterest are wedding day highlight reels, blogs and magazines give increased visibility of high profile, and often high budget, weddings and the expectations that come from family and friends can make it all seem unbearable.

Let's set the record straight. The perception of perfect is different for everyone and for us, a perfect wedding is a wedding that ends in a marriage between two people who are wildly in love and have chosen to make the commitment, together.

The amount of money you spend doesn't matter, your guest list doesn't matter and those tiny details you stayed up nights thinking about; they don't matter either.

Embrace imperfectly perfect, because there isn't such a thing as perfect. Know that things will pop up on your day that were unplanned, or not accounted for, and that is totally okay. Real weddings are just that, real. They have budgets that are often not infinite, real family drama, real weather and real guests who each have their own personality.

In the lead up to the wedding take time away from the pressures of social media. Like we said; it's a highlight reel and often doesn't expose the things that haven't gone how the wedding day spreadsheet said it should.

Take inspiration, absolutely, but don't try to replicate.

Keep in mind that styled shoots are styled. A team of creatives have spent a whole heap of time, often in a controlled environment, putting together something that is 'picture perfect' and these shoots often aren't able to be emulated in a real wedding setting.

Remember that other people's weddings might have had huge budgets, twice or three times bigger than what you were hoping to spend . And sometimes photographs often do not tell the story about a family member who is noticeably not in attendance because of their stance on marriage equality or that there was a tear in a dress as a marrier was getting ready that had to be temporarily pinned together for photos.

Things are bound to go 'not according to plan,' and that should be half the fun.

Remove the stress of 'you only have one wedding day' and think about why you're choosing to marry, it's about marriage and not a wedding. The quality of your marriage doesn't depend on the party you were able to throw for your loved ones, nor does it lie on the quality of the table napkins.

We've said it twice, and we will say it one thousand times over, take time out in wedding planning to read just bearings, especially if you loose focus. It's easy to be consumed in the pressures of perfect when you're consuming wedding media everywhere you go- trust us, we know. Date your lover, ban wedding talk and remember why you love one another enough to choose the rest of your lives together.

And, when the day rolls around, be in the moment. If things don't go quite to plan, like a rain storm rolls over minutes before your outdoor ceremony or their caterers car breaks down on their way to the venue and they are running two hours behind, know that everything will be okay.

The world works in mysterious ways when it comes to things like that, it'll all work out. Maybe the clouds will part and a rainbow will shine over your nuptials. Take a deep breath, hold one another and remember why you're all gathered- to celebrate your love story.

Let your love celebration be 'imperfectly perfect' in every way.

CAROLINE & NERGIS | LOVE IS ART
Photography by Caitlin Taylor, Coral Dove Photography
www.coraldove.com

We met online on OkCupid. Apparently, we were a 75% match which has been enough to make a lifetime of memories and laughter. We met in person for the first time in Bar Louie in Rockville, Maryland. Caroline invited Nergis to her then works happy hour and we have been in each others lives ever since.

Our favorite memory together was the Light Festival. It was our first trip away from the kids after our seconds birth. Caroline had planned a surprise getaway in Harrisburg, Pennsylvania.

We began our way to the festival where they have live music and incredible food. Throughout the day we had discussed our visions of the future and everything aligned as we light up our lanterns and they became one with the atmosphere. On the lanterns we wrote about the things we loved about one another- it was one of the most romantic nights we have shared.

"My favorite thing about Caroline is that she has the best sense of humor. I love that she can make me laugh and doesn't take life too seriously. She is also very empathetic, which is something that we share. Her ability to give and help others is so inspiring."
- Nergis

Being an inter-racial lesbian couple has been one of the most defining aspects of our relationship.

People are always curious about how women from an Islamic and Catholic background can both live authentically as ourselves in a same-sex relationship and live our lifestyles. Although we don't practice any particular religion anymore, we feel that our relationship breaks so many different barries and proves that love prevails regardless of cultural or religious background.

We have observed others from various cultures and backgrounds full of curiosity openly admit that we have changed their perceptions about non-traditional families.

Nothing is sweeter to our ears than that.

"My wife's mind is ever growing. She is knowledgeable beyond her years and I find that fascinating and sexy. Yes, she is beautiful and an amazing dance partner, but she is so caring and extremely humble too."
- Caroline

For us, our biggest challenge of being together has been bringing together our two fur babies. We both had dogs before we started dating and unfortunatly they have not always got along. Initially, we were breaking up small dog fights! Funnily enough, they are now best friends and we often find them cuddled up together.

Our future looks adventuresome yet humbling. We're planning to add another baby to our family of four and complete some potentially big home renovations. We also can't wait to travel more together. Nergis might go to grad school, but that is still up in the air.

EMMA & NICOLE

PHOTOGRAPHY BY TAHNEE JADE PHOTOGRAPHY
www.tahneejadephotography.com

DRYSDALE, AUSTRALIA

find your seat

One morning Emma and Nicole lay in bed musing about life together. Emma turned to Nicole while eating honey toast and said 'let's get married!', Nicole said 'yes!', and the two lovers were engaged.

With memories together of lazy afternoons under the fruit trees, a family property, sentimental to Emma and Nicole, on the Bellarine Peninsula was host to their special day.

From early on in the planning, Emma and Nicole knew that they wanted their wedding to feel like a warm hug. Magical, festive and uplifting with an earthy, Australiana palette. They wanted their guests to relax, indulge in incredible food and cocktails and enjoy the beautiful surrounds as they danced the night away.

And it's exactly that experience that the lovers were able to bring to life.

Emma, who happens to be very gifted at finding images and visual references, found Nicole's dream wedding dress. For Nicole, it was a surreal moment when she first saw it; it was as though her ideal wedding dress had magically come to life. The red Steven Khalil gown was inspired by the universe and cleverly named the Burgundy Universe Gown.

For Emma finding the perfect outfit was more spontaneous. Working long hours in the lead up to the wedding meant that she wasn't able to physically go shopping, instead, she ordered something she loved online and crossed her fingers that it would fit- thankfully, it did.

Choosing to get ready together, with their newest family member, Fern, a ragdoll kitten, Emma and Nicole walked into marriage as a team.

Emma and Nicole both feel elated by the experience of their vows and the ceremony. Having the opportunity to look back into the loving faces of their family and friends while making their promises and commitment to one another, was unforgettable. It was that magic, at that moment, that they will cherish forever.

And, for Emma, there was a surprise during the vows. Nicole had a wooden park bench created by her Step-Father as a wedding gift to Emma, complete with their names etched into the wood.

The brides opted for more of an unconventional rather than a traditional wedding, with all focus on doing things their own way. They stayed together the night before the wedding, had their Mothers walk down the aisle together who were then followed by their Fathers. They didn't do a 'first dance' instead, they had a musical serenade. Nicole, who is a professional singer, sang a few love song dedications to Emma that were followed by some other special guest performances.

The wedding had a relaxed flow, the intention of the newlyweds to create a magical and spontaneous energy.

Although there was some wedding planning stress they each made a conscious effort to pause for moments throughout the day to just enjoy what they had created. It was a decision to relinquish control and embrace whatever unfolded on the night, which made for some wildly fun experiences surrounded by their nearest and dearest. The evening made just that little bit more magical when it was revealed that Nicole had organized a surprise fireworks display. The perfect start to the next chapter of their lives together.

Catering Truffle Duck | **Celebrant** Jo Betz | **Chair Hire** Elderberry Events | **Cinematographer** Little Cinema | **Entertainment** Chela, Steve Clisby, DJ Whiskey Houston | **Event Planner, Florist, Hire & Stylist** The Hattie and Bairn Tribe | **Gown Designer** Steven Khalil | **H&MU** Taryn Harvey, Chiara Tripodi **Jacket** Vintage Piece | **Lighting & Sound** AVFX Melbourne | **Menus** Paperlust **Napkins** Event Art | **Neon Sign** Neon Collective | **Pants** Versace | **Photo Booth** Zuster Photo Booths | **Photographer** Tahnee Jade Photography | **Place Cards** Crafted Signs | **Rugs & Cushions** Nomad Styling | **Seating Signage** Crafted Signs | **Shirt** Versace | **Shoes** Dolce & Gabbana, Gucci | **Tipi** Hire Tipi Tribe | **Venue** The Whiskery

UNDERWATER LOVE
Photography and Words by Robyn Nicole Film and Photo
www.robynnicolefilmandphoto.com

I met Danielle and Phoebe through an unlikely scenario involving contra dance and a long-winded meeting at an underground [literally] bar over drinks and was immediately dazzled by their love. In a real way.

There's a sort of starry-eyed that happens to your face when it's confronted with completely unattainable, staged, poised, expensive love, and then there's the sort of starry-eyed that I felt when, sitting across the table from the two of them in the dim light, I could just feel that they were the sort of people that go home every night and rub each other's feet. They probably wake up early just to watch each other dream, I thought. They probably scratch each other's hard-to-reach-itches and tweeze the hard-to-see-spots of each other's eyebrows. Whether or not any of this is true is, of course, is yet unknown, but I could tell that they had an honest and serving kind of love and I was mesmerized.

When they asked me to be their photographer, I was beside myself with excitement, and when they told me that they wanted to celebrate their love during the course of an entire weekend, I had to motion toward the defibrillator near the doorway.

Danielle and Phoebe did what I implore all humans celebrating love to do-they threw a damn party, and they packed that party with all of their favorite things, a list that could only be satisfied by a long weekend away at camp. Their dear friends and family packed into the sweet little cabins of Maine Teen Camp for three days of karaoke, crafts, dancing, a movie screening, lawn games, shared meals, campfires, and playing in the lake.

Danielle and Phoebe did a remarkable job of stitching together many of their favorite activities into a weekend that everyone close to them could also enjoy. It was fantastic for me as a photographer to be present long enough over the course of three days to see people really relax and grow toward one another. Each morning brought progressively tousled heads bobbing toward a sleepy breakfast together, and each night, they shared

laughs at the day's hijinks over s'mores on a fire.

When a short portrait session in the surrounding forest was punctuated by frequent stops to spot mushrooms that caught Danielle's eye and that she called by name, I was overjoyed to be able to sit in that space without feeling rushed by the usual schedule of things.

Phoebe and Danielle stand out to me because they queered their wedding in so many more ways than one. They were playful in their planning and made decisions that put themselves and their friends and family well ahead of normative expectations of a celebration of marriage. They gave themselves and everyone around them time to bask in the true phenomenon of love in all its varied forms. They threw a damn party.

There is so much more I could tell you about; three days is a lot of time to pick up on a lot of different things. Most notably, I suppose was that Danielle made her own bouquet. She is an extremely skilled and creative floral designer at a Portland, Maine greenhouse that gets a lot of less-than-creative work thrown its way, so she was more than fired up to create for herself a loud, unapologetic, and carnivorous masterpiece. She grew the pitcher plants herself and added a hidden owl charm to the side of the bouquet that she held nearest to herself in remembrance of her late mother.

Another notable and beautiful event happened about a week before their wedding weekend when I, on a whim, texted the two of them asking whether or not they might feel like jumping into the lake after their ceremony. I wouldn't mention it, of course, if they hadn't replied with a unanimous and resounding YES, and I hadn't the pictures to prove it.

These two are just fantastic, and other such people deserve the chance to look outside the predictable, linear, 8-10 hour weddings that we inherited in the fight for marriage equality.

WAYS TO WALK DOWN THE WEDDING AISLE

From five couples that have done it

Ari & Lucy

We didn't put a lot of thought into who would go first. In fact, we can't actually ever remember having a conversation about it until our wedding officiant asked us about two weeks out from the wedding date!

For no real reason, other than Lucy putting her hand up first, Lucy walked first with her Mom, and Ari followed with both of their parents.

Sarah & Sarah

Sarah R cringed at the thought of walking down the aisle. Her parents have unfortunately been unsupportive when it came to her marrying Sarah and the tradition just brought up too much emotional angst. So, Sarah R waited at the altar under our beautiful copper and floral arbor [that she built herself!] and Sarah W walked toward her arm in arm with her Dad.

It actually worked out great because it meant that Sarah R was there to greet guests and share the rollercoaster of excitement and nerves with all of our guests and Sarah W, who has a tendency to always be late, had an extra minute [or twenty!] to finish getting ready.

Meaghan & Kate

We actually both walked down separate, but at the same time! Instead of having one walkway down the center of the ceremony venue we opted to have two walkways cut through our seating arrangement.

We were incredibly thankful to have the support of our parents and we both walked down with both of our parents! We know not every venue can cater to the way we had it set up, but it was so perfect for us.

Rosie & Sky

We were so indecisive about who would walk first, and then second, so we went about it in an unconventional way. We started our wedding morning together [with a celebratory champagne breakfast, of course] and tossed a coin before we separated to get ready with our respective wedding parties. We actually kept it a secret from our guests right up until the

last minute! Rosie ended up walking down first with her younger brother and Sky walked second, by herself. Sky had always wanted to walk alone because to her it signified an independent woman making the choice to commit to her bride for the rest of her life.

Unconventional, sure, but it was the perfect solution for us.

Lara & Nicole

We decided early on [if we are honest before we were even engaged] that we would have a 'first look' at our wedding. So, after we had our first look, and we had a chance to wipe away all the happy tears, we had our photographer invite our parents in to share a special moment together before we wed.

Our parents each walked us to the top of the aisle, said their congratulations, and we walked the rest of the way together.

Suzy & Ryn

Neither of us walked down the aisle.

When it came to wedding planning every single decision, including decisions to include more traditional elements, was matched with us asking ourselves and each other why we wanted to include it. We had a small and intimate wedding of just 23 of our closest friends and chosen family, neither of us liked the idea of being 'given away' and having an entrance just wasn't important.

Together we greeted our guests as they arrived to the ceremony and when the time came our officiant announced the start of the ceremony to us all. We simply walked up to the front of the room from where we were standing at the time and everything began after everyone found their seats.

Although we hadn't heard of other couples doing it the same way as us, we knew it was perfect and right for us.

HELLO, SHANNON STENT IMAGES
Contributed by Shannon Stent, Shannon Stent Images
www.shannonstentimages.com

Who is Shannon?

I'm a photographer living in the coolest place on earth, Cowaramup, in Western Australia.

I freaking love my job. It has allowed me to meet some incredible people and travel to some wild places. I also love the ocean; it's where I go to recharge and it's my main source of positive energy and creativity.

I have a perfect little family that means the world to me and I'm grateful to be able to work alongside my partner in crime, Jayde, every day.

Where does your passion for both photography and videography come from?

I've always been fascinated with the ocean and capturing its moods. I was first drawn to the video side of things, chasing waves all over the place. When our first daughter Coco came into the world, I found a new passion for capturing people and relationships.

How would you describe your style?

Raw, natural, atmospheric and moody.

How do you feel about pre-wedding or engagement shoots?

Personally, I love them! It's a great way to get to know people to and be a little more creative without the pressure of wedding schedules and bridal parties.

What is your best advice for couples who are choosing their wedding photographer?

When choosing your wedding photographer, you first need to determine the style of photography that you love. It all comes down to personal taste.

The next step is to arrange a face to face meeting with your potential photographer to dicuss your wedding photography in more detail, and you'll soon figure out if this is the person that you want sharing the biggest day of your life with you. It is absolutly important that you feel comfortable in their company.

How many photographers should couples have on the day?

From our experience, and in my opinion, two sets of eyes are better than one. We photograph and video our weddings with two photographers or videographers. For us, it means we can capture your day from a variety of angles and means no important moments are missed!

You get to travel and capture love around the globe, what's one destination that's at the top of your wish list? And, why?

I've always wanted to visit and photograph Iceland. I know that it may be a little clichè, but I'm all about those wild landscapes. Drop me on a black sand beach with all the ice and all the wind [and a couple of lovers] and I'd be loving life!

ERICA & LEAH

PHOTOGRAPHY BY GEORGIA WIGGS PHOTOGRAPHY
www.georgiawiggsweddings.com

ST KILDA, AUSTRALIA

For Melbourne locals, Erica and Leah, when they met through mutual friends almost six years ago, it was love at first sight. They have been inseparable ever since.

On an anniversary trip to Port Douglas to celebrate five years together, Erica stopped by a picturesque tropical green oasis by the water. While soaking up the sunshine she gave Leah a custom made '90s View Master' complete with two photo reels that told the story of their last five years together. The very last slide was an image of handwritten words that told Leah how Erica felt about her and how much she was loved. When Leah took the camera from her eyes Erica was down on one knee and asked; 'will you be my wife?'

Both brides-to-be wanted a venue that would tick every box, rather than having guests travel about different locations. They stumbled across the Harbour Room and the 180-degree views of St Kilda and the Melbourne Skyline, matched with the green marble bar and rooftop had them sold. The venue already had incredible views and so they'd have the option to stick to minimal styling; simplistic yet stylish.

Dress shopping was as laidback as the couple. At the very first shop they stopped by, Luv Bridal, they each chose three gowns to try on. The first dress Erica tried on ended up being the one Leah would fall in love with for herself, and Erica couldn't imagine anything more perfect than the second gown she tried on. Both dresses, with lace that complemented the other perfectly, were locked in, orders placed, all within the hour.

From the beginning stages of wedding planning, it was important to the brides to never compare their wedding to others, or any expectations. They took the time to pat themselves on the back for the incredible planning, budgeting and teamwork that made their wedding day come together and knew that all their guests wanted to see was two women both smiling on their wedding day.

And, that almost carefree approach flowed right into their wedding day.

As excitement built, so did the nerves. Erica and Leah chose to get ready together. They were able to wake up next to each other and calm each other's nerves and also there to relish in every moment of excitement. Details that made everything just a little bit more magic.

With their 'Bride Tribe' in tow, the lovers took the time before the ceremony to have couples portraits around Fitzroy, determined not to miss a moment of celebration, or any cocktails, after the ceremony. It was a choice that they would recommend to other couples who also don't want the stress of having to leave and come back to the ceremony.

They wed on the rooftop and everything was perfect. Having so many family and friends there to witness, share and approve of their love was something that will always stay close to Erica and Leah's hearts.

And, in true Erica and Leah style, an epic party [passionfruit mojitos included] flowed well into the night.

To the newlyweds, marriage means communication, teamwork, love, romance, laughter, and trust. It's being comfortable enough to let someone see all your flaws, your goofiness, and your fears and giving one person the blessing to enjoy all the laughter, accomplishments, unconditional love and every part of you; be it good or bad. To Erica and Leah, they are that person to each other- for a lifetime.

Accessories ASOS, The Iconic | **Bridal Boutique** Luv Bridal Moonee Ponds | **Cake** Ayse Ali | **Catering** Food and Desire | **Celebrant** Katie Clayton, Happily Ever After Celebrant Services | **Ceremony & Reception Venue** Harbour Room, Royal Melbourne Yacht Squadron | **Entertainment** DJ Alana McLeod **Florist** Chloe Lashay Floristry | **Flower Girl Outfits** ASOS | **Gown Designer** Madi Lane | **Hair** Brittany Cartel | **Makeup** Mandyn Nicole Makeup Artist, Sandra | **Photographer** Georgia Wiggs | **Rings** Windfall Jewellery | **Robes** Boohoo | **Stationery** Zazzle | **Transport** Kombis I Do

HELLO, MY WEDDING CELEBRANT

Contributed by Kitty Kulman, My Wedding Celebrant
www.myweddingcelebrant.com.au

Who is Kitty, the creative lady behind My Wedding Celebrant?

I wear so many hats.

Firstly I am a mum to two young children and recently became a wife to my long term partner, Andrew. I have a background in science and got into weddings to fulfill the creativity that I had bottled up for years.

I am a bubbly creature attracted to anything that sparkles, and I love more than anything to have a laugh. I have a kind nature and try to help couples have a stress free ceremony, using my project management skills to take care of everything and anything ceremony related.

What does being a Wedding celebrant [or officiant] mean to you?

As a wedding celebrant, I get to be a marriage maker to everyone - how incredible! Love is love right, and I believe any two people in love should be able to show their commitment to each other in front of all of their favorite people.

But it is also a little more than that. Being a wedding celebrant, I get to set the tone for the amazing party that follows after the ceremony.

When did you find a love for the wedding industry?

After I made it though my first wedding. It was a rainy day in Perth and I was with the couple, their dog and their two witnesses - super intimate and beautiful. But, I got such a thrill. I was hooked after that. I love being able to support and provide couples a way to get married how they want to.

You attend so many weddings, what's your favorite part of the wedding day?

The ceremony, of course! There is no better opportunity to set the tone and have everyone feeling those warm and fuzzy feelings.

Give us your best wedding advice.

The day goes SO fast. Honestly, people will tell you that it does and they are telling the truth. Take time just to pause and just soak it all in.

Reconnect with your partner during the party and just enjoy it. Things will not go exactly to plan but what does it matter? You just married the love of your life and what could be better than that?!

What has been a standout, favorite moment, of being a Celebrant?

I was going to perform a commitment ceremony for two ladies. And, because of marriage equality laws changing, I was able to ring them and let them know it could now be a legal ceremony.

They were so happy and grateful, and it was amazing to help them get married.

JAMIE & MADELEINE

PHOTOGRAPHY BY STORIES BY BIANCA
www.bianca.co.nz

KAUKAPAKAPA, NEW ZEALAND

Jamie and Madeleine's love story starts in a unique way. They met through work, but were working in different company offices; Jamie in Auckland, New Zealand, Madeleine in Brisbane, Australia.

Their friendship grew over the course of a year, but developed into a long-distance romance as real feelings started to be shared. From there, quick overseas weekend trips were regular until Jamie decided to jump the ditch and relocate to Australia.

The pair were engaged for a little more than two years.

Wedding planning was smooth sailing even though it would be the first time that the two families had come together. It made perfecting the seating plan just a little bit harder.

They decided to wed in New Zealand since they now live in Australia. Waterfall Farm the perfect host to a wedding that would have a wedfest, boho feel about it. Minimal styling needed, the landscape and surrounding nature painted the most impeccable backdrop.

For both Jamie and Madeleine, it was imperative that they held a wedding that was as environmentally friendly as possible, conscious of the waste that is often created from just a single day celebration. The couple opted for reusable linens, palm leaf plates, and compostable utensils and chose a florist that works sustainably using local growers and suppliers.

The wedding was a mostly DIY affair; in fact, only the structural and furniture components weren't. Madeleine made homemade Mazavaroo Chilli as wedding favors for each guest. Together the couple hand sowed over 40 meters of bunting and Jamie carefully handwrote all of the wedding stationery and signage. Friends and family also helped bring

the wedding day to life, Madeleine's sister, Emilie, spending eight hours creating a custom art piece and an incredible friend, Jodi, who spent more than 26 hours creating a magical macrame arch.

For Jamie, there were multiple bridal boutique visits before she found herself letting go of 'dress anxiety' at a Grace Loves Lace showroom. For Madeleine, it was evident that a custom suit would be the best option from early on and opted for a dark green that complimented the wedding day in every way.

When the wedding day came around it was everything that the couple had imagined, and then some. Having their families unite for the first time, from across the world and various parts of New Zealand was a gift they will forever cherish.

Walking back down the aisle, after long and heartfelt vows, hand in hand as wife and wife for the very first time, another unbeatable feeling.

The ceremony, the reception, the slightly awkward first dance and the laughter that erupted when the newlyweds tried to cut the cake with a tiny wooden knife because they'd forgot to bring anything else; every moment was authentic and as beautiful as the last.

For Jamie, marriage is about finding the person you fit perfectly with, even though there isn't a perfect relationship or person. It's about how you work together, laugh together, and help each other be better versions of yourself. For Madeleine, it's finding the person that is your family, your home, your love. And for both the newlyweds, it's finding the mother to their future children, the person you want to adventure with and grow old with. Someone that they will always have fun with, cry with and laugh with.

Accessories Ruby & Sage, Off Ya Tree | **Bridal Boutique** Grace Loves Lace | **Brides People Outfits** Evolution NZ, Tree of Life, Billy J | **Cake** Daisy Cakes Auckland | **Caravan Bar** One Little Wagon | **Catering** Sadie's Table | **Celebrant** Bell's Celebrant Service | **Ceremony & Reception Venue** Waterfall Farm, Kaukapakapa | **Decorative Elements** Palm Leaf Plates | **Event Planner & Stylist** DIY, Blume & Darling | **Florist** One Poppy | **Food Trucks** Cook at Home Paella | **Furniture Hire** assembly. | **Hair** Rachel Haaker | **Makeup** MP Makeup | **Marquee** Party Hire Auckland | **Photo Booth** Snapshot Station **Photographer** Bianca Hawk | **Prop Hire** Joho Creations | **Shoes** London Dune, Brogues | **Socks** Happy Socks | **Suit Designer** Germanicos | **Tie & Bow** Tie Otaa | **Veil** Rue de Seine | **Wedding Rings** Angus & Coote

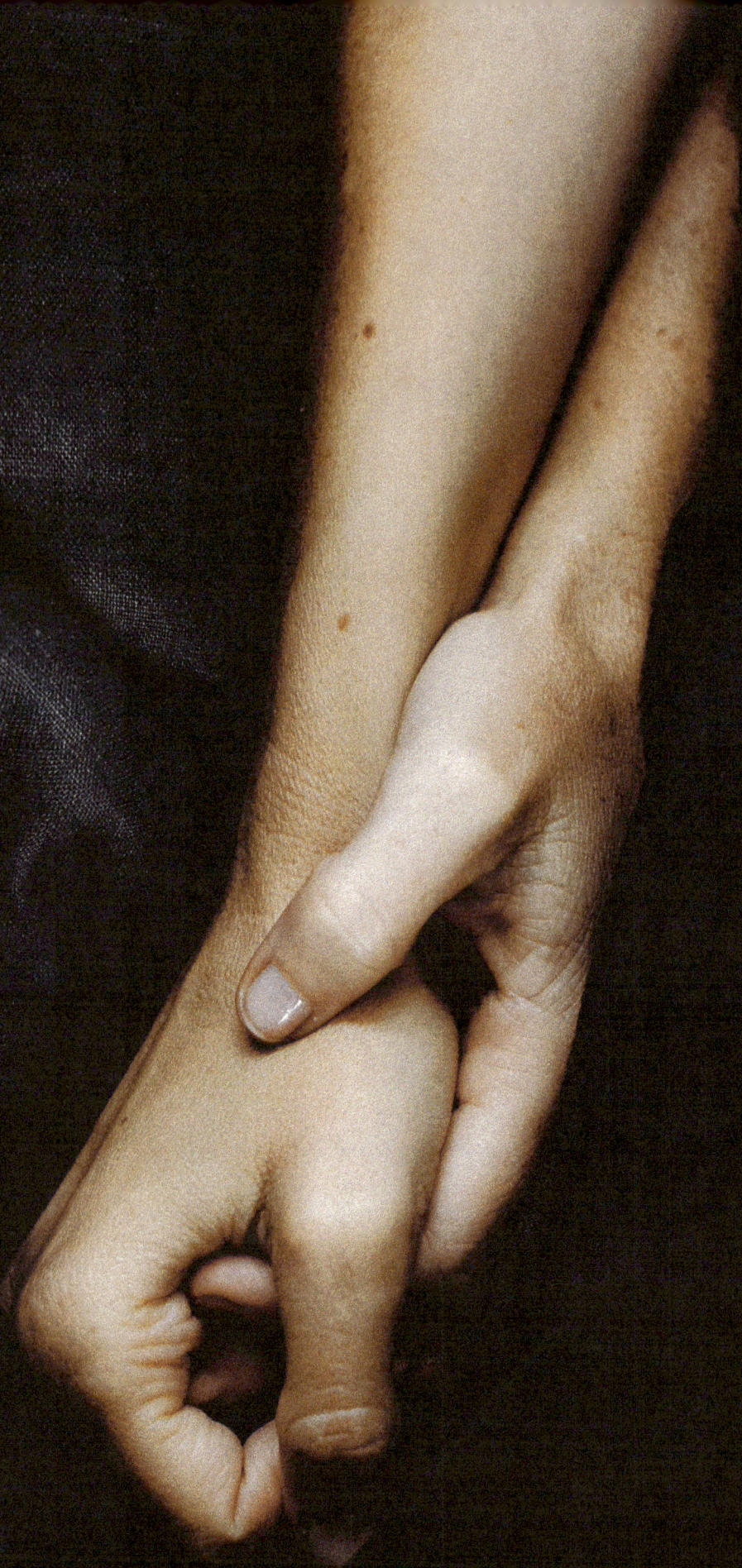

These are the songs that brought the weddings featured in this
edition to life.

This Will Be	**Natalie Cole**
Sure Thing	**Miguel**
Simple Things	**Miguel**
Save a Little Love	**Don Diablo**
Chateau	**Angus & Julia Stone**
Special	**Six60**
Crazy Love	**Van Morrison**
Halo	**Beyonce**
You've Got the Love	**Florence & The Machine**
Something About You	**Odesza**
I Found You	**Benny Blanco ft Calvin Harris**
Jurassic Park Theme Song	**John Williams**
Summer	**Calvin Harris**
I'm With You	**Vance Joy**
Kiss Me	**Ed Sheeran**
Your Song	**Ellie Goulding**
Firestone	**Kygo**
I Love You Always Forever	**Betty Who**
The Woods	**Hollow Coves**
Mango Tree	**Angus & Julia Stone**
Teenage Crime	**Adrian Lux**
Forever You and Me	**The Teskey Brothers**

Live by the Sun –
Love by the Moon

Celebrant Kirk Goodsell Celebrant | **Creative Direction** Duo Events Creative Studio & Ridhwaan Moolla | **Design, Styling & Florals** Duo Events Creative Studio | **Food Styling** Duo Events Creative Studio & Kerstee | **Furniture, Tablecloths, Black Glasses** Hire Society | **Hair** Emmanuelle Helena | **Jewelry** Bianko | **Lovers** Kate & Clare | **Macarons** May Street Larder | **Makeup** Rachael Forster Makeup Artistry | **Outfits** Maevana Bridal | **Photography** Ridhwaan Moolla | **Stationery** Paper Fusion Boutique | **Tableware** Side Serve Perth | **Venue** Nature Inspired Eco-House | **Vases** Curio Warehouse

A styled shoot allows a creative team of vendors bring to life a concept that they dream of creating. This edit was no different. A team of creatives from a range of educational, cultural, body and sexuality diveristies showcased lovers, Clare and Kate in this modern elopement.

What was the inspiration behind the shoot?
We really wanted to showcase that an 'elopement' is about how a couple intentionally and intensely celebrates their love and commitment to one another. A day just for them.

In order to make this poignant, we decided that there needed to be a narrative to the shoot – highlighting and showcasing each moment of love and connection. Starting with the initial tender moments of waking up in the morning, to getting ready, the ceremony, the intimacy of dinner and then falling asleep at the end of the night.

We framed the shoot entirely around 'connection' – deciding that a minimal but animated style would be the best way to not only showcase a different way to celebrate but also bring the focus clearly back to what it is about at the end of the day – a 'distinct' kind of love.

Describe the style of the shoot?
A key element of the shoot was to emphasize the passage of time and the transition between periods of an elopement day. We chose to do this visually with a strong contrasting palette of only white and black. Commencing with a calm white on white morning, then moving to a more energetic mixed white and black afternoon, followed by a rich and embracing black on black evening look.

Our connection with white was centered around calmness, purity, and safety. We wanted the morning to start with a fresh wash of white – representing a fresh start and a trusting bond between two people.

To introduce the black transition we had Kate gift Clare with a black Pomeranian puppy called Fiddy Scent, a really special way to introduce energy and a pop of celebration to the day.

As the day transitioned we introduced more black to bring in a level of formality and refinement, the mixed white and black palette was dedicated to the getting ready, ceremony and couple portraits sections of the shoot. As a team we wanted to focus on strong forms and simple structures. It was important for the imagery to be strikingly different with juxtaposed elements while at the same time having Kate and Clare incredibly connected throughout the images. This ensured that the focus was purely on their connection.

We chose an inner-city house just outside the Perth CBD that has beautiful textures, a neutral palette and lots of natural light. We also chose this location to demonstrate to couples they can have a beautiful elopement in their own city!

As a conclusion to the elopement we wanted to have both Kate and Clare in all black enjoying an intimate dinner for two [of course with all black foods!] We truly wanted to showcase the beauty and drama of a monochromatic palette, whilst depicting a luxurious, intimate setting for two.

How would you sum up the edit?
Warmth, love, and many joyous squeals of excitement!

As vendors, watching Clare and Kate was an absolute joy and a privilege. They were so full of affection, so authentic and revealed how much love they had for one another over the course of the day. We watched them be totally connected with each other every minute, a hard task with ten sets of eyes on them!

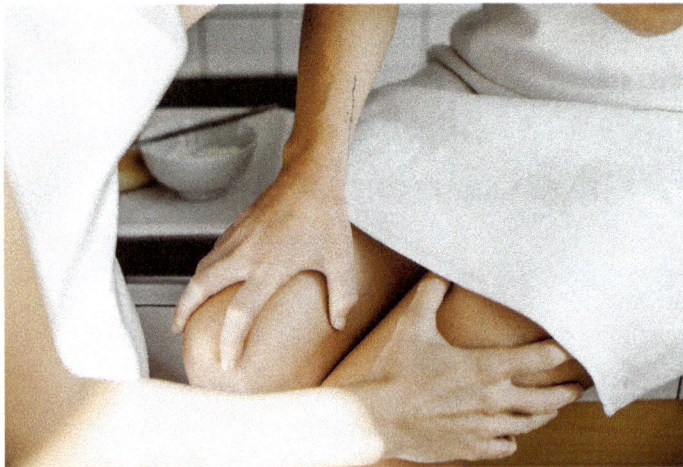

HER

WEDDING VOWS

JESSICA & SARAH

PHOTOGRAPHY BY EMILY HOWLETT PHOTOGRAPHY
www.howlettphotographyweddings.com

CARLSRUHE, AUSTRALIA

A romance blossomed between Jessica & Sarah on the dancefloor of a Melbourne nightclub. The moment Jessica walked on to the dancefloor, the rest of the club, and all eyes were on the platinum blonde in the blue dress who was dancing like no one was watching. Jessica told Sarah that she was beautiful, and they spent hours together dancing into what would be a brilliant romance.

While they had initially wanted a long engagement, while researching venues they came across Hedge Farm in central Victoria. The venue only had one weekend available for next year, so the lovers locked it in.

Wedding planning had its ups and downs. There were times where they found themselves correcting wedding vendors who made assumptions that they were having a 'double wedding' and times where they found themselves talking about ridiculous things that held a weight of importance - like whether they needed 100 pieces of fudge or 150. Something they giggle back at now.

The sensible, and frugal, couple took on a few DIY projects for the wedding day. Together they created a candy bar for guests, picking up different sized jars on weekend shopping trips for the weeks leading up the wedding. They created their own 'thankyou' bags to complete the bonbonniere. Sarah also created confetti cones with old books and collected handkerchiefs from op shops for the 'tissues for the happy tears' basket.

The wedding vibe was boho meets bush, meets festival vibe into the night. Hedge Farm's natural beauty drawing in the couple from the moment they laid eyes on it. The atmosphere created not just by the native greenery and pops of deep reds, but too by musician Simon Paparo [who

was found by the couple busking on the streets of Melbourne] who played acoustically for the first half of the celebration.

With the guest's comfort and experience at the top of mind, Jessica and Sarah had planned a quick ceremony; it took just 15 minutes to wed legally.

Sarah arrived in a vintage Valiant with her Mum and Dad, and hid in the bush until Jess and her Mum walked down the aisle. Sarah walked second, arm in arm with her Dad to the Jurassic Park theme score.

Introduced as 'the newlyweds, Sarah and Jess', food, drinks, and celebrations followed.

Sarah and Jess didn't have a wedding party, rather, they opted to have their closest friends and sisters sit on the table with them, wearing whatever they felt most comfortable in. It was essential to the couple that everyone was able to express themselves authentically and enjoy the day fully.

Sarah and her father took dance lessons and had a Father-Daughter dance to 'Little Ray of Sunshine'- the same song that had played on the radio on the way home from the hospital after Sarah's birth. Jessica and Sarah had also taken dance lessons and put what they had learned into practice to "I'm With You" by Vance Joy. Their first dance as wife and wife.

Guests let their hair down, both on the dancefloor and in the Kombi photobooth provided by The Photobooth Girl. They also had the chance to devour sweets from the Brulee Cart, a very welcome addition to festivities.

Bridal Boutique Always and Forever Bridal | **Catering** Going Gourmet | **Celebrant** Love Your Way Celebrations | **Ceremony Venue & Reception Venue** Hedge Farm | **Decorative Elements** About Flowers Kyneton | **Desserts** Going Gourmet | **Engagement Rings & Wedding Rings** Melbourne Jewellery Service | **Entertainment** Simon Paparo | **Food Truck & Cart** El Paletero, The Brûlée Cart | **Makeup** Chelsea Darnell- Makeup Artist | **Photo Booth** The Photobooth Girl | **Photographer** Emily Howlett Photography | **Shirt & Suit** Politix | **Signage** Vistaprint | **Sound Hire** Melbourne DJ Hire

Run away with me.

PHOTOGRAPHY BY KAMRA FULLER PHOTOGRAPHY

www.kamrafuller.com

Words by Kate Faoro Wright, Tapestry Event Company & Runaway With Me Elopements

Melissa and Tamara met at a gym in Des Moines where Melissa was the General Manager. Tamara's first thought upon meeting Melissa was, "Hey! That's nice customer service." Melissa took the time to notice people both as they walked in the door and as they left, or so Tamara thought. Little did she know that Tamara was one of the most striking people Melissa had ever seen but was too intimidated to approach. Cut to a couple of years later and a new city, Tamara was Melissas 'gym crush' that she was fated never to see again; until Tamara walked through the door.

Melissa recounts numerous embarrassing attempts to talk to her, including walking her to the locker room, yelling awkward goodbyes as she was half-way out the door, picking up trash conveniently around the club to 'randomly' fall into conversation, letting Tamara's son into the kids club for free, and saving Tamara's number in her phone 'just in case.'

Soon after, Tamara came up with a plan to see if Melissa was into women by sharing that a male 'friend' was into her, to which Melissa quickly called Tamara out on her story. Eventually Tamara worked up the guts to call the gym one day and get Melissa's number. They went and got drinks the next night; then the next, and the two nights following that.

Within a month, they had spent every single day together and told each other they loved each other. Within two months, they had moved in together.

Two years later, they decided to marry the woman of their dreams.

Tamara was first drawn to Melissa for her maturity, the way she cares for other people, and her sense of independence and assertiveness as a woman. She is constantly in awe of Melissa's capacity to love and build a life together. Melissa frequently creates opportunities to treat Tamara to experiences she would never create for herself or put off in favor of others. Tamara is always learning how to strengthen relationships with those that love back, and say goodbye to those relationships that no longer serve, by Melissa's inspiration.

Melissa was struck by just about everything in Tamara, but especially the way she treats the people in her life with respect and a boundless capacity to forgive. She frequently hears Tamara say to her son, "I love you more than I love myself" and that is the epitome of that phrase. Melissa is most proud of Tamara for growing a firm set of boundaries to balance her ability to love and forgive. Melissa is also consistently inspired by their ability to value independence in balance with the solidarity of their relationship. They are allowed and encouraged to live their own lives while making joint decisions and sharing an empathic listening and experience of life.

When did Tamara know that she wanted to marry Melissa? "I chose marriage because honestly, one day, I was watching her cook and all I could think is, 'Never let her go.' I wanted to always wake up to her, be able look at her, know she's mine and know I'm hers. I finally had that feeling that I wasn't missing out on anything, never wondering if there was someone better for me. I love the feeling that I get from the thought I have when I know I'll love her forever and ever."

Why did Melissa choose marriage with Tamara? "Because I value her enough to commit every day of my life to bringing her up. Because I am a better person with her and she is a better person with me. We both deserve to have that, forever."

Together, these women support each other's growth by being an unfailing source of encouragement and support for one another. If Melissa has a long day at work, Tamara steps in unprompted by cooking dinner, cleaning the house, and setting up home life so that Melissa can arrive and relax. By listening to one another and never putting the other down, they can communicate with one another clearly, be heard, and make decisions as a team.

They both agree that the love they share is something they've never experienced before. It is from this place of faith in their love that they are both looking forward to expanding their family and sharing the experiences of raising a child, progressing in school and their careers, and buying a house together. As these two brave, beautiful women continue to walk the path of in-vitro fertilization to expand their family, they are committed to tackling big decisions by listening to each other's opinions and ideas first.

They are more than partners; they are soulmates, best friends, and represent all the beautiful forms of strength and stability that a marriage needs.

Accessories ASOS | **Collective** Run Away With Me Elopements | **Design & Planning** Tapestry Event Co | **Dessert** Sift and Gather | **Dress** Rue De Seine Bridal, The Dress Theory Seattle | **Fiber Artist** Mosshound Designs | **Floral** Villanelle Floral | **H&MU** Holly Tipp Makeup | **Jumpsuit** ASOS | **Lovers** Melissa & Tamara | **Photography** Kamra Fuller Photography | **Stationery** Sable Wood Paper Co

CLEO & LIV

PHOTOGRAPHY BY CLOUD CATCHER STUDIO
www.cloudcatcher.co

KIRRA, AUSTRALIA

Welcome

TAKE A DRINK 🍷
&
← PICK A SIDE. →
EITHER WAY,
you're with the

···bride···

(please put your phones away
during the ceremony and
be present with us in the moment)

♥ Cleo · Liv

There had been a lot of talk about getting married, but no real plans were made, at the time same-sex marriage wasn't legally recognized in Australia. Liv was sure that Cleo would hold off until it was legal and was completely surprised when Cleo did propose at a local surf competition. She'd even organized a long lunch with both their families later that day to celebrate.

Cleo grew up on the Gold Coast, and together these two Brisbane lovers knew that it was essential to be by the ocean on their wedding day.

Kirra Hill was the perfect spot; with an incredible view and a casual DIY vibe which allowed Cleo and Liv to make their wedding entirely their own.

There were a few 'non-negotiables' that the brides-to-be discussed leading into their wedding day. The wedding had to be a big party, nothing too formal or structured, and there had to be an outfit change leading into the reception because neither bride felt that they could really get down on the dancefloor in long gowns.

Indecisively, Liv brought three wedding dresses, two pairs of earrings, two pairs of shoes and a jumpsuit in the lead up to the wedding. Although the outfits were kept a secret between the brides until the day of the wedding, both had brought their reception outfits from the same store. Cleo opting for a twin set muted floral short and blazer combination, and Liv a white one-shoulder jumpsuit.

The day before the wedding was spent together, with the wedding parties, creating native bouquets together and sipping down a few sneaky champagnes.

On the wedding day, Liv woke at 5 am to watch the sunrise from the beach, evident from that moment that the day was going to be perfect.

The couple had time for a quick cuddle in the morning before heading off to get ready separately with their wedding parties.

Their first look was out the front of the La Costa Motel, the same motel they had rented out in its entirety for guests who had traveled interstate or internationally to be there for the day. It was the moment that they both describe as the most special, a moment that cleared any nerves that either of them had about what was to come.

Both Cleo and Liv walked down the aisle with their Dads, Cleo first and then Liv. Vows were personal and intimate, and surprisingly quite similar considering neither knew what the other had written. While neither couple, or respective families, are particularly religious, it was important to Cleo and Liv that they pause to mention absent friends and loved ones during the ceremony, and again during the reception, that were unable to be there.

After promises were made for the future, and a kiss to seal the deal, guests were treated to an incredible grazing table, canapes, gelato, cake, and donuts. The newlyweds taking off for a quiet moment by the ocean with their photographer, Cloud Catcher Studios.

As the sun set, the party was just getting started. The now barefoot newlyweds and guests celebrated this epic love tale and new commitment well into the night stopping briefly to devour a three-layered chocolate, gingerbread and coconut cake made lovingly by Liv's Mum and Sister.

While the day was a whirlwind, Cleo and Liv's advice to couples planning their own wedding is to take the time to really enjoy being engaged. It's just one day and there isn't any need to make everything absolutely perfect or to do things a certain way. Don't worry about what you should do; just focus on what you want to do.

And so the Adventure begins

CLEO & OLIVIA
6TH OF APRIL 2019

Cards
& WELL WISHES

Catering See You Next Thursday | **Celebrant** Haylea Gorton | **Ceremony Venue & Reception Venue** Kirra Hill Community & Cultural Centre
Cinematographer Fable House Films | **Desserts** Wheel & Spoon, Krispy Kreme | **Engagement Rings** CTJ Diamonds and Jewellery | **Entertainment** DJ
Gazah | **Event Planner & Stylist** Champagne & Confetti Events | **Flower Girl** Outfits Arabella & Rose | **Flower Wall** The Petal Prop Co. | **Hair** Mhair.
The Salon | **Lighting** Neon Republic | **Makeup** Blush & Bangs | **Marquee** Event Marquees | **Photographer** Cloud Catcher Studio | **Signage** DIY, Etsy
Wedding Rings Secrets, The Gentleman's Smith

ALBERT TSE
METALSMITH

A modern take on the traditional
www.alberttsemetalsmith.com

THE LIST

SOME OF THE VERY BEST WEDDING VENDORS

AUSTRALIA | USA | AROUND THE WORLD

THE LITTLE PRESS
Stationery

We are a design and letterpress studio, creating invitations with a sense of magic and wonder in the beautiful, tactile details. We hand-feed each sheet to our antique presses; a focus on attention to detail. We are for the dreamers, and the wild hearts, who want their wedding stationery to set the tone of their unique wedding day.

www.thelittlepress.net

KOMBI KARTEL
Photo Booth

Meet Bot, a 1961 VW Kombi with a photo booth built right in his caboose. Bot loves to travel from the Sunshine Coast through to Byron Bay and anywhere in between. With glamorous flower walls and hilarious props, Bot is bound to impress all of your guests [even old Aunt Merill].

www.kombikartel.com.au

FIONA CLAIRE
Attire

Inspired by the perfect fit, designer Fiona Green draws on over 15 years experience in the bridal, retail and fashion industries, to create effortless silhouettes for the elegant, modern bride and staying true to Fiona Claire's signature silk fabrications and superior fit.

www.fionaclaire.com

CLOVER CULINARY PROJECTS
Catering

While we do offer easy to navigate wedding packages, we are also happy to custom design menus and drinks offering to suit our couples individually. We love working together with our wedding couples to create an offering based on what they love to eat!

www.cloverfood.com.au

AUSTRALIA

E.G.ETAL
Jewellery

Now in its 20th year, e.g.etal represents and celebrates Australian contemporary jewelry. Each piece is handmade by an individual artist: carefully conceived, beautifully crafted, and sincerely passed on. Choose from an evolving collection of inspiring pieces from over 65 designers.

www.egetal.com.au

SHANE AVE
Attire

Shane Ave provides high-quality custom made formal wear that our clients have chosen and designed to their liking. We offer a variety of fabrics and designs that allows our clients to select colors and fashion that expresses who they are and validate their identity.

www.shaneave.com

KINGS & THIEVES
Photography

We are award-winning chroniclers of humans in love. We are proudly supporting love in all forms. We produce powerful, emotionally-driven work that you'll connect with for years to come.

www.kingsandthiev.es

BAKER BOYS BAND
Entertainment

The Baker Boys Band are live music experts and party starters, infusing every event with energy and full dance floors. Their customizable band size allows you to find the right fit for your style & budget. See them perform live!

www.bakerboysband.com.au

CALDER PHOTOGRAPHY
Photography

I am Aneisa Calder. An adventurous wedding and elopement photographer! I am here to tell your story - the real, raw, gut-busting laughter, the ass grabbing PDA, the things that made you fall in love with each other. That is what I love to capture for you. Let me tell your love story!

www.calderphoto.com

SWEET CRUMB CAKERY
Cakes & Desserts

Sweet Crumb Cakery was first established in May 2014. We are a home-based business in Orange County dedicated to providing delicious and modern buttercream cakes for all your special occasions. Erika's passion and creativity make for a perfect combination to fulfill your every need and craving.

www.sweetcrumbcakery.com

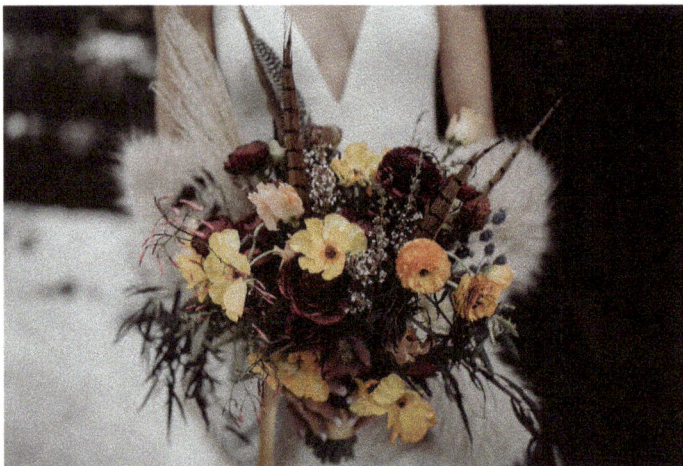

EARTH WITHIN FLOWERS
Florist

We are a seasonally inspired florist based in Northwest Montana. We prioritize sourcing from local farmers and harvesting from natural areas. Melissa, the owner, loves to share the symbolism behind the blooms by incorporating her background in herbalism, flower farming, and native plant studies in her designs and teaching.

www.earthwithin.com

HUNGRY HEART INK
Stationery

I once heard a phrase that went a little something like this, "the only difference between an empty room and a party is an invitation." Let's make that party happen, your way. I make offbeat invites for the offbeat couple, but also on-beat invitations for the on-beat couple, if you know what I mean.

www.hungryheartink.com

Rock & Stone Weddings
Planner & Design

Our passion is creating contemporary and creative weddings and elopements that break some of the tired old rules and look damn fine doing it! Our focus is on experience, yours & your guests. If your ideal wedding is original, a little quirky and a whole lot of fun, you're probably in the right place!

www.rockandstoneweddings.com

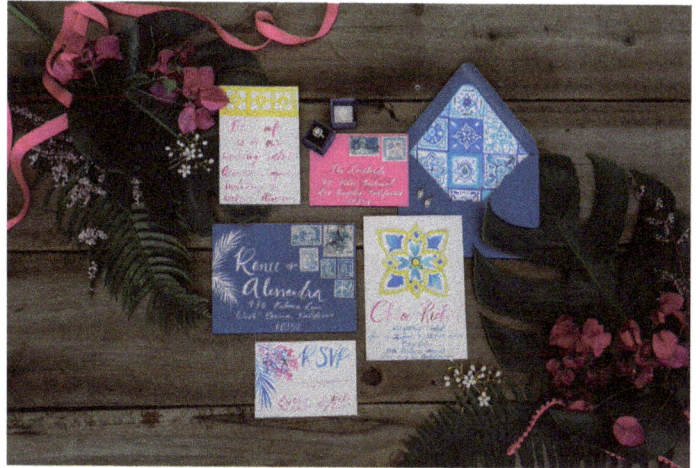

PIGMENT & PARCHMENT
Stationery

Love stories are the main stories she tells with her business, Pigment & Parchment, where she creates bespoke hand painted wedding stationery. Eternally optimistic, Pigment & Parchment artwork is always happy & bright. It seeks to bring smiles to faces all over the world.

www.pigmentandparchment.com

DEVOTED TO YOU
Planner & Stylist

Devoted To You is a team of women, led by Melissa Crawford, that believes in authenticity, individuality, and fun! Carrying those concepts over to the wedding planning process and partnering it with out of the box thinking, helps us to create kick-ass celebrations and unique experiences for every couple.

www.devotedtoyouevents.org

LEX & THE LOTUS PHOTOGRAPHY
Photography

I've had the absolute honor of being trusted by clients turned friends, to photograph one of the most important days in their lives, even in unique destinations like Italy, Japan, Lake Tahoe, and Hawaii. Now grab hands and let's create those romantic, timeless moments TOGETHER!

www.lexandthelotus.com

BOHOTANICAL
Styling & Florist

BOHOTANICAL specializes in boho-inspired wedding styling, as well as dried and faux floral arrangements. I have a strong eco-conscious approach to all my work, ensuring that your wedding day will not cost the earth in any sense!

www.bohotanical.co.uk

FINN & THE FOX PHOTOGRAPHY
Photography

Badass photography for wild souls. I'm Hannah – a sunset geek and a lover of natural light and intimate elopements. I love LOVE, I love LAUGHTER, and I love the OUTDOORS. Planning anything unconventional, alternative or even geeky – I am your girl!

www.finnandthefoxphotography.co.uk

DAISY BRIDES
Attire

Look beautiful, feel comfortable, and reflect your unique style and personality - that's what Daisy Brides is all about. Gorgeous, affordable gowns, with a twist. From classic styles to edgy modern looks, there's something for almost every bride and body type, because all people deserve to feel amazing on their wedding day.

www.daisybrides.co.nz

COUPLE CUPS
Photography

Couple Cups is a Wedding and Portrait photographer based in Hawaii. We live, we wander, we laugh, we love, and we capture the moments that count in pictures that make you remember.

www.couplecups.com

AROUND THE WORLD

FOE & DEAR
Jewelry

Foe & Dear is a collection of one of a kind pieces that are assembled to order by hand and heart. Our jewelry is made with the environment in mind; using recycled or fair-trade gold and conflict-free stones. Each Foe & Dear piece is designed and handcrafted in Vancouver, Canada.

www.foeanddear.com

CHELSEA WARREN PHOTOGRAPHY
Photography

Hi, I'm Chelsea. Sunseeker, light chaser, capturing adventurous couples in the PNW. Wildly creative and always up for a good laugh. I often hear feedback that I feel like and old friend, and I adore that! Come as a client, leave as a friend.

www.chelseawarrenphotography.com

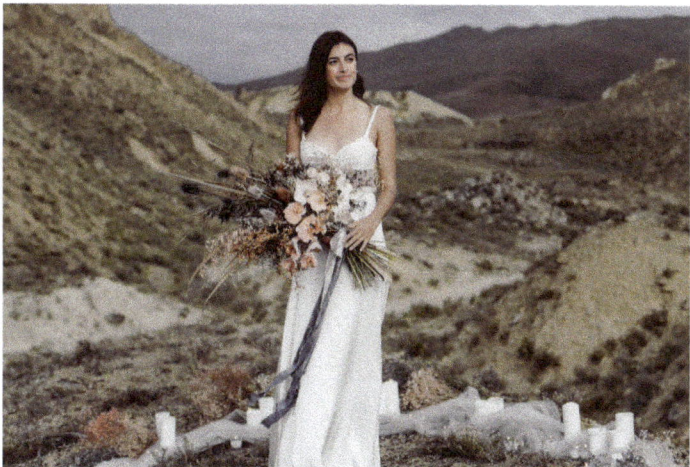

THE LOVERS ELOPEMENT CO
Elopements

We are a collective of creative romantics based in the untamed mountains of Queenstown, New Zealand. We craft intimate and soulful elopements for couples who set their own style. We're bringing back the romance. The Art, the passion, the ritual. The chance to run free from fuss, fanfare, and formality.

www.theloverselopementco.com

BUTLER & WHITE
Planner & Stylist

Authentic & purposeful design is at the heart of everything we do! Creating unique meaningful experiences for people in love is a joy and our mission always. We walk on the wilder side and specialize in elopements and intimate gatherings that embrace the beauty of the natural world where ever your love takes us.

www.butlerandwhite.com

Photo by Gold and Grit

PRECIOUS CELEBRATIONS

. FUN & FIERCE WEDDING CELEBRANT .

www. preciouscelebrations.com.au

@ preciouscelebrations

A SPECIAL THANKS

Dancing With Her couldn't exist without an incredible network of humans from around the globe who support the publication. Whether you follow along on social media, have picked up a copy at a local store or you've found us on the world wide web, we are so grateful that you are here.

This list isn't exhaustive, but it is those who directly contributed to bringing this fifth volume to Dancing With Her magazine to life- it really couldn't be without them.

ARI & LUCY

CAROLINE & NERGIS

CLOUD CATCHER STUDIO
www.cloudcatcher.co

CORAL DOVE PHOTOGRAPHY
www.coraldove.com

EAGER HEARTS PHOTOGRAPHY
www.eagerheartsphotography.com

EMILY HOWLETT PHOTOGRAPHY
www.howlettphotographyweddings.com

GEORGIA WIGGS PHOTOGRAPHY
www.georgiawiggsweddings.com

KAMRA FULLER PHOTOGRAPHY
www.kamrafuller.com

KATE FAORO
www.runawaywithmeelopements.com

KITTY KULMAN
www.myweddingcelebrant.com.au

LARA & NICOLE

MEAGHAN & KATE

MADELINE KATE
www.madelinekate.com.au

TAHNEE JADE PHOTOGRAPHY
www.tahneejadephotography.com

TALITHA CRAWFORD PHOTOGRAPHY
www.talithacrawfordphotography.com

RIDHWAAN MOOLLA
www.ridhwaanmoolla.com

ROBYN NICOLE FILM AND PHOTO
www.robynnicolefilmandphoto.com

SHANNON STENT
www.shannonstentimages.com

ROSIE & SKY

STORIES BY BIANCA
www.bianca.co.nz

SUZY & RYN

...AND ALL OUR MARRIED LOVERS

THE DIRECTORY

A CURATED COLLECTION OF INCLUSIVE WEDDING VENDORS FROM AROUND THE GLOBE

www.dancingwithher.com/directory

HONEYMOON

A COLLECTION OF UNIQUE HONEYMOON OPTIONS
FROM AROUND THE WORLD

JULY

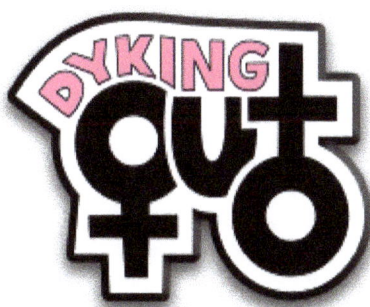

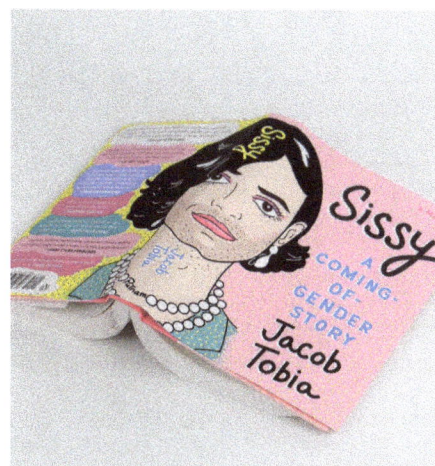

'MUST PACK' CARRY ON ITEMS

BOSE QuietComfort 35 Wireless Headphones *$349* **-** If you're planning on taking any public transport, you'll want to make sure you've got something that will help you block out the world around you.

que Bottle *$24.95* - Not all re-usable water bottles are built the same, and when you're travelling these silicone collapsible bottle [that are BPA free] are perfect! que also donate to environmental charities and that fills our hearts.

Odd Pears *$19.00* - A comfy outfit is essential, comfy and stylish socks are just as important - trust us! These socks not just come in creative patterns and bright colors but they come in sets of three because we all know one will always go missing.

Black Chicken Remedies Nasalettes *$19.95* - Travelling can induce anxiety and these little tubes of goodness filled with essential oil blends are an absolute must have.

PODCASTS TO LISTEN TO

Dyking Out NYC comdians tend to have a way with words and these hosts are no exception. Be prepared to explore femme visbibility, threesomes and dating the 'straight girl'.

To L and Back If The L Word changed your life, this podcast is for you. Leading into the newest season, this podcast deep dives into every single episode that has been made, so far. Kinda like a book club for a television show that connected queer women around the globe.

Homoground More of a music lover? This podcast shares stories of queer artists from around the world.

Food 4 Thot These multiracial queers deep dive on the issues that matter; love, relationships, sex, race and identity.

Busy Being Black Josh Rivers hosts this incredible and thought provoking podcasts that starts taboo-breaking conversations. Think loneliness, shame, stigma and mental health.

SOMETHING TO READ

High School by Tegan & Sara *$29.95* **-** Hands up Tegan & Sara devouts...we knew we weren't the only ones! They're about to bring out a memoir and you can bet a dollar that we've ordered a pre-sale copy.

Pet, by Akwaeke Emezi *$17.99* - If fiction is more your style then this creative story about a monster searching trans gal is bound to have you step out of reality.

In The Deep End, by Katie Davies *$25.00* - This book wil have you in stitches! It's a raunchy lesbian comedy, a little Amy Schumer-esque.

Sissy: A Coming of Gender Story by Jacob Tobia *$26.00* - This book isn't just for the gender-queer. Everyone can learn from this non-binary human and their relationship with gender.

Black Light: Stories by Kimberly King Parsons *$15.00*- This colection of dark short stories are poetic and ferocious.

Santori is the most famous island in Greece, by far, and it is for a good reason. Home to the iconic white buildings and dramatic cliffs this centuries-old city has so much to do, so much to see and so much to celebrate.

While you won't necessarily find dedicated LBGTQ+ hotspots, the community is widely accepted. In fact, same-sex unions have been legally recognized here since 2015.

The best time to visit Santorini is between late April and early November when the weather is warm, and there is little rain. The weather is most temperate between June and September, the nightlife incredible and every opportunity to sunbathe, wine and dine. You will, however, find July and August is the busiest - if you don't like crowds or peak prices best to steer clear of those months. The official language of the island is Greek, but thanks to the tourism English is also widely spoken and understood.

GETTING THERE

Depending on the season you will be able to fly into Santorini from selected European cities, or from Athens year round. One thing you should keep in mind is that the airport can get really busy- so allow extra time to navigate it, especially when you're leaving the airport. Don't forget to ask your accommodation if your stay includes transfers- most do!

On the island, you'll be able to get about by the local bus, a much cheaper option than catching taxi's, or you can hire a four-wheeler bike or small car. The later is the best option if you're hoping to explore secluded beaches and places a little less traveled.

And, because you would be cutting your experience short if you didn't, you can travel between the beautiful islands by ferries that frequently run from their ports.

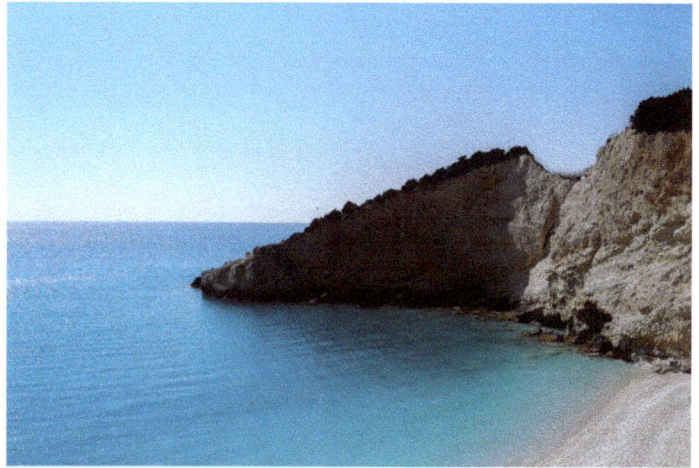

WHAT TO DO

In a nutshell; soak up the sunshine, explore, wine and dine.

Our first suggestion would be to hire a bike or car and find some beaches. Because of volcanic activity around the islands, and Santorini literally is a dormant but active volcano, their beaches are unique and spectacular. Some will have black sand, others white and some even red. With access to transport, you'll have the opportunity to explore tiny pockets of coast that won't be littered with other tourists- bring on secluded beach vibes!

If your adventurous and up for a 10km [or 6 mile] walk, walking from Fira to Oia via a carved out path between the two towns, is a once in a lifetime type experience. You'll walk through small villages and traverse incredible cliffs stopping by plenty of perfect Instagram spots along the way. Hot tip: the Santorini sun can be harsh, pack plenty of water and sunblock.

If Nea Kameni and Palea Kameni weren't already on your bucket list, add them. With steaming hot sulfur springs and natural thermal mud baths it's a pampering day like no other! We can guarantee that this is a memory that you'll always reflect back on fondly.

And, because Santorini is such a tourist hot spot it can be easy to forget that there are locals that live their day to day lives in this incredibly scenic place. Pyrgos is far less visited by tourists than Santorini village but gives you a unique glimpse into how the locals live. It's a charming inland village, off the beaten path and miles from the ocean. It's quiet, whitewashed hilltop village is lined with homes and churches that were built in and around a Venetian castle. The paths are tiny and windy but can be explored for hours and the food scene here is rated the best in Greece. Think fresh salads, tomatoes, and seafood- delicious.

WHERE TO STAY

Essentially you have two choices in Santorini; you stay in resorts, or you stay in quirky little spots- both have incredible hospitality. Here are some of our accommodation options;

Something a little cheaper - *Try Airbnb*

There are some adorable, and very affordable Airbnb's if you love the idea of staying a little more like a local. Honestly, some of the stays available are out of a magazine; the iconic Greek architecture, hot tubs and ocean views are a real treat.

Prices start at around 50€ per night.

Something a little more - *Astra Suites*

Perched atop the volcanic cliffs the Astra Suites are your own personal paradise. The panoramic views of the Aegean Sea, and unparalleled views of the famous Sanorini sunset- and the Astra Suites is currently ranked in the top 25 hotels in the world

Prices start at around 300€ per night.

Going all out - *Ikies*

With just a handful of rooms and honeymoon suites, and a signature breakfast served to you on your own private terrace, Ikies will bring a whole new element of romance to your honeymoon. If you're feeling extra luxe, you can upgrade to their honeymoon package and really feel like royalty.

Prices start at around 350€ per night.

WHAT TO EAT & DRINK

Prepare to be spoilt for choice. Santorini is full of fresh unique vegetables and plenty of fresh seafood. Here's a few place you'll want to add to your list of musts when you visit the island.

Seaside Santorini - Focused on Mediterranean flavors but in a gourmet setting these chefts bring different styles of cooking from all different parts of the world. The stuffed vine leaves are a perfect appetizer.

Catch - If you haven't had the potato gnocchi from Catch, you haven't lived. Also the Dakos, which is a greek version of a cheesecake ir ridiculously addictive, you might want to book for a second night.

Theros Wave Bar - Is one of the best spots for cocktails by the ocean, the Humuhumunukunukuapua'a [yes, that's the real name] a delight

TRYP
Brisbane, Australia

With its modern design, striking art by world acclaimed street artists, TRYP Fortitude Valley Hotel is Brisbane's most exciting hotel stay. Located on the city fringe in the heart of Brisbane's entertainment and nightlife precinct, TRYP Fortitude Valley offers travelers the ultimate boutique hotel experience.

www.trypbrisbane.com

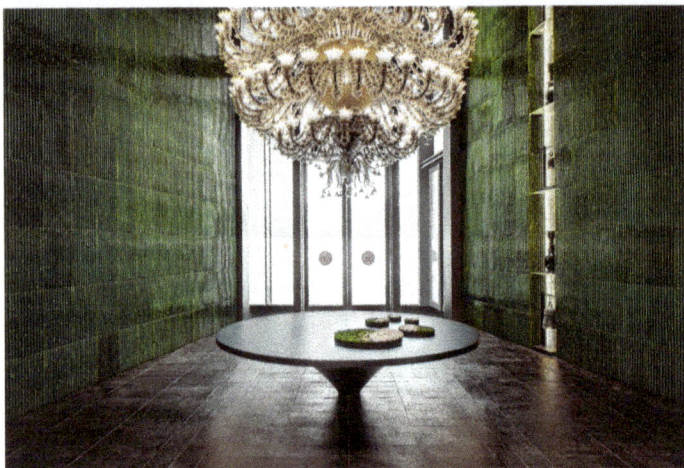

THE MIDDLE HOUSE
Shanghai, China

Located in the bustling Jing'an District of Shanghai and the city's trendy Nanjing West Road, The Middle House is the newest addition to Swire Hotels' renowned The House Collective, offering 111 luxuriously designed guest rooms and 102 serviced residences for discerning world travelers.

www.themiddlehousehotel.com

HOTEL MONVILLE
Montréal, Canada

Ideally located, Hotel Monville is in the heart of Montréal and a short distance from Quartier des spectacles. A 20-story hotel that stands out thanks to its location as well as its new-generation concept and its urban Montréal-inspired decor. Laid-back. Design-minded. Tech-savvy. Always friendly. Monville is Montréal!

www.hotelmonville.com

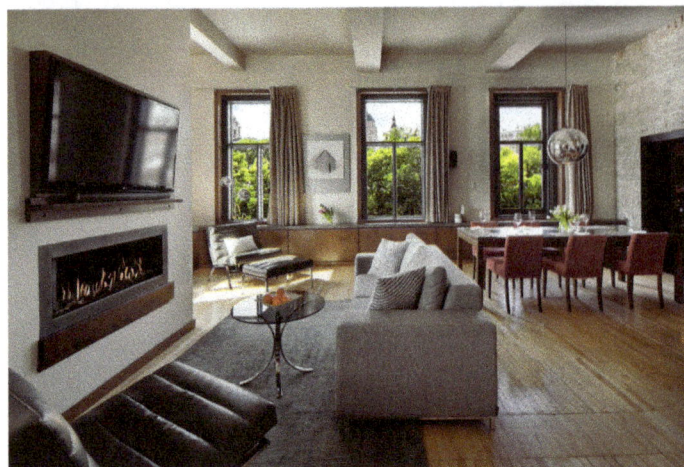

HOTEL 71
Québec City, Canada

Are you looking for a place with an authentic Vieux-Québec vibe? Hotel 71 offers an atmosphere enhanced with the amenities of a 4-star hotel. Luxurious and intimate Hotel 71 offers 60 rooms with sweeping views of Old Québec, the mighty St.- Lawrence River and Cap Diamant.

www. hotel71.ca

ACCOMMODATION

THE WILLIAMSBURG HOTEL
New York, USA

Designed by London-based design firm Michaelis Boyd Studio (Babington House UK, Soho House Berlin), the hotel's 150 rooms and public spaces feature white-washed walls, luxe marble, double-height ceilings, Art Deco-inspired furniture, and sweeping views of the East River and Manhattan.

www.thewilliamsburghotel.com

THE BENJAMIN
New York, USA

Preeminently located in Midtown East, The Benjamin offers an authentic NYC experience with spacious rooms and suites. Thoughtful services and amenities include the Les Clefs d'Or Concierge, The National Bar & Dining Rooms, spa services by Sanatio Spa, and comprehensive sleep program by Dr. Rebecca Robbins.

www.thebenjamin.com

ARLO SOHO
New York & Miami, USA

Nestled beside Soho, TriBeCa and the West Village, Arlo SoHo is an ideal home base for urban explorers. The 325-room hotel offers ample public space paired with cozy, thoughtfully-designed guest rooms. The property also provides a range of food & beverage venues and two inviting bars; Arlo Lobby Bar and Arlo Roof Top.

www.arlohotels.com/arlo-soho

THE

**Williamsburg
Hotel**

@ wburghotel

www.ingramcontent.com/pod-product-compliance
Lightning Source LLC
Chambersburg PA
CBHW051612030426
42334CB00035B/3499